LIFE DURING THE
GREAT CIVILIZATIONS

Ancient Greece

Don Nardo

BLACKBIRCH®
PRESS

THOMSON
———— ✹ ————™
GALE

San Diego • Detroit • New York • San Francisco • Cleveland • New Haven, Conn. • Waterville, Maine • London • Munich

For more information, contact
The Gale Group, Inc.
27500 Drake Rd.
Farmington Hills, MI 48331-3535
Or you can visit our Internet site at http://www.gale.com

LIBRARY OF CONGRESS CATALOGING-IN-PUBLICATION DATA

Nardo, Don, 1947-
  Life in ancient Greece / by Don Nardo.
    v. cm. — (Life during the great civilizations)
  Includes bibliographical references and index.
  Contents: A land of diverse nations and cultures — Social classes and citizenship —
Families and their houses — Religious beliefs and customs — Greek science and technol-
ogy.
  ISBN 1-56711-741-4
  1. Greece—Civilization—To 146 B.C.—Juvenile literature. 2. Greece—Social life and cus-
toms—Juvenile literature. [1 Greece—Civilization—To 146 B.C. 2. Greece—Social life and
customs.] I. Title. II. Series.

  DF78.N37 2004
  938—dc21   2003008270

Printed in United States
10 9 8 7 6 5 4 3 2 1

Contents

A Land of Diverse Nations and Cultures

The term ancient Greece can be misleading because in ancient times, Greece was never a unified nation or empire. Instead, the region of mainland Greece and nearby parts of the Middle East were made up of hundreds of individual city-states and kingdoms. A city-state, such as Athens, consisted of a central city that controlled the villages and farmland surrounding it. A kingdom, such as Macedonia, was usually a larger state made up of a number cities, all controlled by a king. Whether a city or a kingdom, each of these states saw itself as a separate nation.

Though separate from one another, the Greek states all had a few things in common. Their inhabitants spoke Greek, for example. They also worshipped the same pantheon, or group of gods. In addition, they used the same basic methods of warfare and transportation.

There were more differences than similarities, however. Each Greek state

Ancient Greece

Opposite Page: Athens's central hill, the Acropolis, is covered by the ruins of ancient structures.

developed its own form of government. Some were democracies, in which the people ran the government. Others were ruled by councils of elders or by kings. Also, each Greek state issued its own coins and evolved its own local laws, social customs, and attitudes toward women, slaves, and foreigners.

Partly because of these political and cultural differences, the Greek states often quarreled among themselves. These disputes led to many wars that kept them almost perpetually disunited. Eventually,

This ancient Athenian coin shows an owl, symbol of the city's patron goddess, Athena.

in the second century B.C., the Romans took advantage of this weakness. Powerful Roman armies conquered the Greek states and incorporated them into the mighty Roman Empire.

Long before this defeat, however, an enormous cultural flowering took place in Greece during its classical age, which lasted from about 500 to 300 B.C. Athens, in particular, produced a burst of magnificent art, architecture, sculpture, literature, and philosophy that awed succeeding generations.

This happened partly because Athens was a democracy that encouraged and inspired artists and thinkers. It was also a naval power whose people traveled widely and developed relations with many foreign lands. The rival city of Sparta, by contrast, was a military state ruled by a council of elders and two kings. Sparta emphasized soldiering and war rather than art and culture. For a long time, it had no navy, distrusted foreigners, and rarely traveled beyond its own borders. Everyday life in Athens, therefore, differed in numerous ways from life in Sparta. This book looks at aspects of both societies during the classical age.

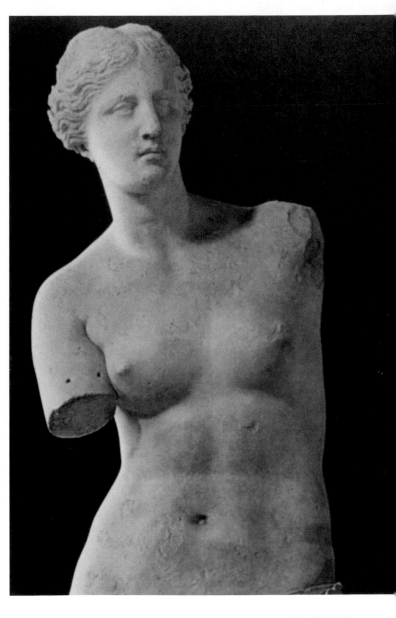

This statue of a goddess is one of many surviving art treasures from ancient Greece.

CHAPTER ONE

Social Classes and Citizenship

One factor that all of the ancient Greek states had in common was the importance they placed on citizenship. As a small, distinct nation in its own right, each developed great pride in its local way of life and was ready to fight to protect it. To be a citizen of such a state was seen as a great honor, therefore. For that reason, much of the social structure of a typical Greek community was built around either the possession of citizen status or the lack of it.

For most of the Greek states, the exact breakdown of social classes and qualifications for citizenship are uncertain because very little information about politics and society in these states has survived. By contrast, a fairly large amount of data about life in Athens has survived. In the classical age, Athens was large, populous, prosperous, and home to many first-rate writers whose works passed down to later generations. Athens was undoubtedly more successful and accomplished than most other Greek states. Still, modern scholars believe that the basic societal groups in a majority of these communities resembled those in Athens.

The Importance of Citizenship in Athens

Among these Athenian social classes, the most privileged consisted of male citizens. Free adult men who were born in Athenian territory were the only people in the community

Opposite Page: This illustration shows some of Athens's public buildings as they likely appeared in the fourth century B.C.

with full civil rights. They could vote, hold public office, and plead cases in court. They also enjoyed *isonomia*, equality under the law. Most were farmers who owned and worked their own land, but some were merchants and craftsmen.

Less equal under the law were two other groups of free Athenians—one citizen, the other noncitizen. Like their husbands and fathers, free women born in Athenian territory were citizens. They were second-class citizens, however. The Greek term for their special status was *astai*, meaning citizens without political rights, which meant that women could neither vote nor hold public office. Also, a woman was not allowed to bring a case to court on her own. A male relative had to plead the case for her. The law placed other political and social restrictions on women as well. According to one Athenian statute, "the women who come to mourn at the funeral are not to leave the tomb before the men."[1] Also, an Athenian writer stated that "the law expressly forbids . . . women from being able to make a contract

This modern engraving depicts the clothes worn by well-to-do Athenian women.

[about anything worth] more than a bushel of barley."[2]

The noncitizen free Athenians were called *metics*. They were either non-Greeks or Greeks from other states who dwelled in Athenian territory. *Metics* worked mainly as merchants and craftsmen. Some were bankers, metalworkers, or jewelers. Others made and painted vases, cups, and other kinds of pottery. They not only lacked political rights but also could not own land or houses. (*Metics* did pay taxes and serve in the military, however.)

To have full citizenship was therefore a high honor and privilege in Athens. The loss of citizenship, which was a penalty for some crimes, was both a social disgrace and a practical hardship. A person who suffered this loss was called an *atimos*. He was barred from voting or holding public office. He could not enter a temple or the marketplace. If a citizen saw him in one of those places, that citizen had the right to arrest him and turn him over to the authorities.

In this vase painting, two metics weigh rolls of cloth in a fabric shop.

Sparta's Regimented Society

Citizenship was also a major aspect of the social organization at Sparta, an important city-state located about a hundred miles southwest of Athens. Spartan citizens, called Spartiates, made up a small minority of the population. Unlike Athenian men, male Spartiates were forbidden to engage in farming, trade, or other professions. (They owned land but did not work it themselves.) Instead, they were raised from an early age to become full-time soldiers. This is because for a

long time Sparta had Greece's only permanent standing army, which was widely feared.

In fact, Spartan society was built almost entirely around a system that educated and trained young male citizens for the military. This highly regimented, often harsh system was known as the *agoge*. It began when Spartan elders examined male babies to see if they were fit to live. According to the first-century A.D. Greek writer Plutarch,

> The father of a newborn child was not entitled to make his own decision about whether to rear it, but brought it to . . . the eldest men. . . . If after examination the baby proved well-built and sturdy, they instructed the

Working Women in Athens

Some female freed slaves played the flute or sang as a way to earn income.

In Athens and other Greek states, it was socially unacceptable for middle- and upper-class citizen women to work outside the home. In contrast, for poor women to work was both expected and accepted. Everyone knew that they and their children needed the income to survive. Poor citizen women often worked as barmaids or sold bread and other food items in the marketplace. They were also midwives, wet nurses for babies, laundry workers, and textile workers. Female *metics* and freed slaves held some or all of these same jobs and labored right alongside poor citizen women. Former slave women also tended horses in stables, played the flute or sang at dinner parties in wealthy homes, or sold perfume, shoes, and other clothes and grooming items.

father to bring it up. . . . But if it was puny and deformed, they . . . [decided] that the child should [be left outside to] die.3

Those boys who survived this grim test had to leave home at age seven and live with other trainees in military barracks. There, they learned to endure hardships and become tough, skilled soldiers.

The other societal groups in Sparta were far less privileged than the male Spartiates. A male citizen's wife, mother, or daughter was also a citizen. She had no political rights, however. Still, Spartan women enjoyed some freedoms that women in many other Greek states did not. In Sparta, female citizens could own land. They also exercised and played sports alongside the men. This was to keep the women in top shape so that they could bear many healthy baby boys to replenish the army ranks. Sparta also had noncitizen resident foreigners, called neighbors. They lived apart in their own villages. (In contrast, Athenian *metics* often lived alongside citizens.)

This modern painting shows young Spartan men and women exercising.

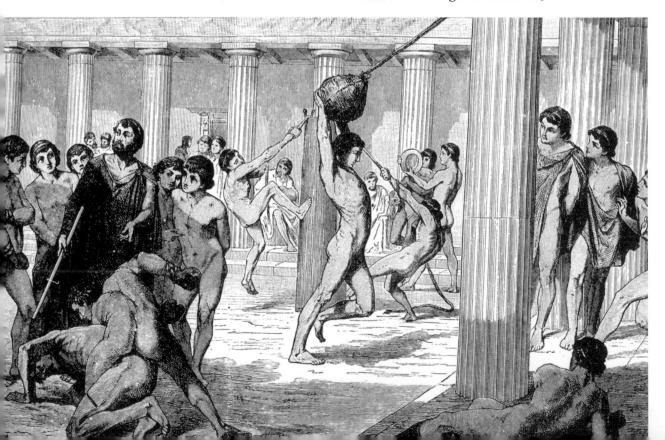

Society's Lowest Class—Slaves

Far below the citizens and neighbors on Sparta's social scale were the slaves, called helots. The helots worked the farms owned by Spartan citizens, which freed the latter to devote themselves to soldiering.

Helots were often treated cruelly. Many were beaten regularly to keep them in a state of fear. Also, as part of their military training, young Spartan men killed and terrorized helots, with the permission of the government.

A slave woman pours wine for a nobleman in this scene painted on a drinking cup.

With some exceptions, the lot of slaves in Athens and most other Greek states was considerably better than in Sparta. Athenian slaves were either war captives or children born of slaves. They numbered about 100,000, a third of the total population, during the classical age. A family of average means kept 2 or 3 slaves. Wealthier citizens and *metics* had as many as 15 or 20 Businesses sometimes had even more, as in the case of a shield-making shop that had 120 slaves.

On occasion, a slave bought his or her freedom or was freed by a kind master. A freed slave did not become a citizen, however. Such a person possessed the same inferior social status as a *metic*. In this way, citizens in Athens and other Greek states carefully maintained their own social superiority and privileged positions.

Husbands and Wives

To make sure that the family survived, the leading male and his wife strove to have at least one son. If they did not produce a son, they often adopted one. The reason for the preference of a male heir was that Athenian society was male dominated. The head of each family was a man. Also, the law ensured that property ownership passed from father to son, not from mother to children. In his own household, therefore, the father was the boss and decided the rules, which other family members were expected to follow.

Spinning and weaving were among many household duties of Greek women.

The average Spartan household was run differently from those in Athens. Most Spartan husbands spent most of their time living in military barracks or fighting wars and were rarely at home. As a result, a Spartan wife usually made the rules and ran the entire household. Such independence often made Spartan women outspoken and strong-willed. According to Plutarch, "Spartan men were always subject to their wives and allowed them to interfere in affairs of state more than they themselves did in private ones."[4]

Although wives outside of Sparta did not make the rules at home, their contributions to the household were vital to its success. They and their daughters made clothes for themselves, the men of the family, and the children. Athenian wives also helped to prepare meals, sometimes paid the household bills for their husbands, and supervised the children.

Children and Education

As a rule, these children were born at home. A midwife (*maia*) delivered the baby with the help of other female family members. Usually, the mother gave birth in a sitting position on a special birthing stool. To follow ancient custom, as the child was born, the women cried out loudly to show their joy. After the birth, the parents announced it to the community by attaching one of two items to the front door. An olive stem signified a boy. A piece of wool meant a girl.

A few years later, it was time for the child to begin his or her education. Boys usually began to attend school at age seven. Such schools were small and private, with teachers (*grammatistes*) paid by the parents. The students learned to read and write. They also memorized verses from the *Iliad* and *Odyssey*, epic poems by the widely revered eighth-century B.C. Greek writer Homer. Often, a household slave escorted a boy to school to ensure his safety and see that he was well-behaved. Meanwhile, young girls remained in the home. There, their mothers taught them spinning, weaving, and other household arts.

A painting shows a Greek schoolboy (seated) listening to a teacher's lecture.

A House—and Its Rooms

During the classical age, a majority of houses in which the children were born and raised were relatively small and had simple layouts. With occasional exceptions, even wealthy Greeks in this period lived in modest, sparsely furnished homes. In Athens and most other Greek states, an average house was erected on stone foundations. It featured walls made of sun-dried clay bricks and was sometimes two stories high. The floors of the rooms at ground level were usually made of hard-beaten earth. It

was common, however, to cover the earth with layers of pebbles or mosaic tiles. Floors on the second story were generally made of wood.

A typical house had a central courtyard that was open to the elements. Most of the rooms in the house lined the courtyard and faced inward to take advantage of the natural lighting. In suitable areas, the builders dug a well in the courtyard to provide the family with a private water supply. Some houses had cisterns, tanks that caught and stored rainwater.

Among the rooms that lined the courtyard was the exedra. This was a sitting area that opened directly into the courtyard. Because it had plenty of fresh air and light, the exedra was one of the more popular rooms in the house. Nearby was the kitchen. It had a raised hearth for cooking, and tables and cupboards for preparing and storing food.

The bedrooms numbered between two and five, depending on the size of the family. The master of the house and his wife occupied one bedroom. (This is the origin of the term *master bedroom*.) The children shared another, although sometimes the eldest son had his own room. The family slaves also shared a bedroom.

When Friends Came for Dinner

In Athens and many other Greek states, some of the better homes had a special room called an *andron*. It was a dining room reserved for

Women Banned from Male Parties

In Athens, women were not allowed to attend dinners and parties given by the father of the house. This was because

A vase painting shows women in their quarters, usually located in the rear of the house.

society frowned on women who mixed socially with men from outside the family. During a party, the women retired to their quarters, located either upstairs or in the rear of the house. When a Roman writer named Cornelius Nepos visited Athens, he thought it was odd to separate men from women this way. He asked,

What Roman would blush to take his wife to a dinner party? It is very different in Athens; for there the woman [of the house] is not admitted to a dinner party, unless relatives only are present. And she keeps to the . . . part of the house called the women's apartment," that no man can enter who is not near of kin.

the father to entertain his male friends. (Women were excluded and had to stay in their quarters.) While lying sideways on comfortable couches, the men enjoyed a friendly dinner, often followed by a symposium, an after-dinner drinking party. It was not unusual for a host to hire entertainers, such as musicians and dancers. Sometimes, though, the men preferred to mix their wine with good conversation. In the *Symposium*, a work by the Athenian philosopher Plato, one man says, "I don't think we need this flute girl who's just started playing. She can play to herself, or to the women upstairs, if she feels like it, but for this evening I suggest that we stick to conversation."[5]

Thus, a Greek home was more than a shelter where family members slept, ate, made clothes, and did chores. It was also a place where a few privileged members of the community gathered for a bit of leisure and entertainment.

Guests at a Greek symposium were served by slaves. This drawing shows a slave boy filling a guest's cup.

CHAPTER THREE

Religious Beliefs and Customs

Most Greeks were devoutly religious, and everyday life was strongly influenced and shaped by religious beliefs and customs. "All men who have any degree of right feeling," Plato wrote, "at the beginning of every enterprise, whether great or small, pray to the gods."[6] Indeed, births, marriages, funerals, meals, travel departures, public meetings, and even battles were always accompanied by some form of religious ceremony.

The Greeks believed that showing respect to the gods in this way was crucial to the welfare of the community. In fact, anyone who openly neglected or disrespected the gods was seen as a potential danger to everyone else. His or her offense could anger a god, who might react by punishing the whole community.

The idea that a god could be either angry or pleased with humans reflected the way people pictured these deities. In Greek eyes, the gods had humanlike bodies, personalities, and emotions. They felt rage, pity, fear, joy, and sorrow. Also, like people, the gods engaged in warfare and made mistakes they later regretted.

There were two major factors, however, that made these beings distinct from humans. First, the gods were immortal whereas humans grew old and died. Second, the gods possessed enormous power, enough to flatten an entire city or unleash a deadly plague on its inhabitants. Comparing mortals to the immortals, the Greek poet Pindar wrote, "From a single mother we both draw breath. But a difference in power in everything keeps us apart."[7]

Opposite Page: This renaissance ceiling painting shows the Greek gods, including Zeus (bottom, with thunderbolt).

This bronze figure of Zeus, leader of the gods, dates from about 460 B.C.

Patron Gods and Their Temples

According to early Greek traditions, the strongest of these powerful beings dwelled at the summit of Mount Olympus, in northern Greece. For that reason, they became known as the Olympians. (By the classical age, people recognized that this was fable and held that the gods lived in a faraway, invisible realm.) The leader of the Olympians, the strongest god of all, was Zeus. His symbols were the thunderbolt and the eagle.

No matter which city or kingdom they inhabited, all Greeks desired to maintain the goodwill of Zeus and his Olympians. In addition, each state counted on the special protection of a particular god. It was thought that this local patron god favored that state over most others. The patron who watched over and aided Athens was the goddess of war and wisdom, Athena. Likewise, Poseidon, ruler of the seas, protected and brought prosperity to the city-state of Corinth.

These gods did not offer such protection and support out of a feeling of duty or simple kindness. Instead, they expected humans to provide various things in return. First, a patron god expected the people of the community to erect a suitable shelter, in the form of a temple, in his or her honor. For example, the Athenians built the Parthenon and Erechtheum. These magnificent temples, dedicated to Athena, stood on

Athens's rocky central hill, the Acropolis. People thought that the goddess resided in these structures on occasion. Therefore, it was important to respect her privacy. For this reason, formal worship of Athena and other deities took place outside, on temple grounds.

Sacrifice

Formal worship was another of the important acts the gods expected humans to perform. The two major aspects of worship were sacrifice and prayer. A sacrifice was a material gift offered to a deity. Most often, animals were sacrificed. The common belief was that this nourished as well as showed respect to the god. Typical animals killed in such ceremonies included cows, sheep, and goats.

The ruins of the Parthenon, greatest of all Greek temples, sit atop the Acropolis.

To perform a sacrifice, the worshippers first hung flower garlands over the animal, which they called the victim. Next, they led the beast to an altar. To purify the victim and altar, to make them clean and acceptable in the god's eyes, a priest or priestess sprinkled spring water over them. Then he or she hit the animal on the head with a club. While the victim was stunned, the person slit its throat with a knife and allowed the blood to drain into a bowl.

Finally, several people used knives and axes to cut up the animal. They burned the bones and some of the organs, which produced smoke. The belief was that the god inhaled the rising smoke, which nourished and satisfied him or her. Meanwhile, the worshippers divided up, cooked, and ate the meat.

Prayer

The other major aspect of worship, prayer, could be either public or private. Public prayers included those said at marriages, funerals, town meetings, and so forth. Often they consisted of a general appeal to the gods on behalf of the community or a group of its citizens. Before the start of a trial, for example, the Athenian orator Demosthenes told the

jury, "I begin, men of Athens, by praying to every god and goddess that . . . they may direct you to such a decision . . . as will contribute to your common honor."[8]

In a private prayer, an individual usually asked a god to grant blessings of some kind. Such blessings might be in the form of material gain, such as money or fame. By contrast, the following prayer attributed to the Athenian philosopher Socrates asks only for wisdom: "Beloved Pan [an important woodland god] . . . give me beauty in the inward soul. And may the outward and inward man be at one. May I reckon the wise to be the wealthy."[9]

When saying such prayers, the worshipper stood on his or her feet. It was considered unseemly for a free person to kneel in prayer. The worshipper raised both hands, with the palms turned upward, and spoke aloud. (A silent prayer indicated that the person had something to hide from other people.)

CHAPTER FOUR

Greek Science and Technology

The ancient Greeks had a burning curiosity about nature and how it works. For this reason, they were the first people in history to develop a modern approach to science. Before the Greeks, the Egyptians and others had devised various forms of mathematics. They had also observed the sky and kept precise records of the movements of the heavenly bodies. These endeavors influenced early Greek thinkers.

What made the Greeks different was that they were more than mere passive observers. They rejected the age-old notion that the stars, planets, and other natural wonders were gods or objects that moved according the whims of gods. Instead, they viewed all of nature as a cosmos. In Greek, this word means an orderly system governed by natural laws. A number of Greek thinkers strove to understand these laws and find out what made the world function. A later ancient writer, Lucretius, wrote,

> When human life lay groveling . . . under the dead weight of superstition . . . a man from Greece was first to raise mortal eyes in defiance. . . . Fables and the gods did not crush him. . . . The vital vigor of his mind prevailed. . . . Superstition, in its turn, lies crushed beneath his feet, and we, by his triumph, are lifted level with the skies.[10]

Greek scientists went on to discover many truths about nature. One thinker, Aristarchus of Samos, argued that Earth travels around the sun, instead of the other way around. Another, Democritus, correctly predicted that all matter is made of tiny particles

Opposite Page: Ancient Greek thinkers strove to understand natural laws, including those that govern astronomy.

called atoms. Still another Greek, Empedocles, proposed that living things evolve and change over time. His theory of evolution was astonishingly similar to the one introduced by Britain's Charles Darwin more than two thousand years later.

In spite of these and other brilliant insights, however, most Greek thinkers confined themselves to theory—the realm of ideas and explanations. Few tried to apply scientific principles in practical ways. The result was that the general state of technology remained primitive. Although the potential existed, Greece never became an industrial society.

Lighting and Heating

No Greek discovered the principle of electricity, for example. That meant that people had to use simpler, less reliable means to see in the dark. One of the more common lighting devices was the oil lamp. It usually consisted of a small, shallow vessel made of pottery, stone, or metal that held a burning wick fueled by olive oil. Torches and candles were also widely used. Sometimes people set several burning candles in a tall, decorative stand called a candelabra. Even with a great many oil lamps and candles, it was still difficult to do close work at night. As a result, diligent Greek readers coined the phrase "burning the midnight oil."

Heating methods were also primitive. The household hearth provided some warmth. People also used braziers, metal containers that burned charcoal. These were usually fairly small and portable, so they could easily be moved from room to room. Greek houses did not have chimneys. Smoke from the braziers had to vent through open windows, which made rooms without windows smoky and uncomfortable.

The round hole in the front of this oil lamp from the fifth century B.C. held the wick.

Finding and Using Water

Another necessity of life, water for drinking, cooking, and bathing, sometimes came from wells and cisterns. These were not always sufficient,

What Is the World Made Of?

Most early Greek scientists believed that the natural world must have a single underlying principle or structure that made it and its many systems function. They called this principle the *physis* (the term from which the word *physics* derives). A Greek named Thales, who lived during the sixth century B.C., proposed that the *physis* is water. His pupil, Anaximander, disagreed. Anaximander thought that beneath the surface, nature is made up of an invisible substance he called the "Boundless." Another thinker, Anaxagoras, suggested that all objects in nature grow from tiny seeds that have existed since the beginning of time. These and several other explanations for the *physis* turned out to be wrong. In contrast, two bold thinkers, Leucippus and Democritus, recognized the true structure of matter. They said that all matter is made up of tiny particles, which they called atoms. Summarizing this theory, a later Greek thinker, Aristotle, wrote,

> According to the theory of Democritus, it is the nature of the eternal objects to be tiny substances infinite in number.
> . . . He conceives them as so small as to elude our senses, but as having all sorts of forms, shapes, and different sizes.

however, especially in large towns, where demand for water was high. One common solution was to build the town beside a river or, preferably, clear mountain stream. The residents erected a fountain house beside the stream. A fountain house often looked like a small temple, with a slanted roof and columns running down the sides. Inside, one or more stone tanks stored water from the stream. People either dipped buckets directly into the tanks or used metal spouts located on an outside wall. In some towns that lacked nearby streams, the fountain houses got their water from aqueducts. These were stone channels that carried water from lakes or streams to a town.

Having a ready source of water was only the first step. People also had to get the water inside their residences or bathhouses. Palaces, large bathhouses, and a few wealthy homes sometimes had their own fountain houses. These often featured pipes, usually made of baked clays, that carried water from a fountain house or aqueduct directly into a bathroom or public shower. Average homeowners could not afford such luxuries. They or their slaves had to lug water home in

Greek women fetched water from fountain houses and carried it home in large vases.

ARCHIMEDES.

buckets and fill their bathtubs by hand. Clay pipes carried away wastewater to sewers, backyards, or fields.

Many Greek houses had toilets, too, usually made of hard baked clay. Pipes carried wastes away to the sewers or sometimes to private stone-lined cesspools. In homes without toilets, people used pots, which they carried outside and emptied. Athens and some other cities also had public toilets. Like private versions, they were equipped with drainage pipes.

The Difficulties of Travel

The necessity of carrying water in buckets emphasizes an ever-present reality of life in the ancient world, Greece included. Almost all work was accomplished using the muscle power of humans or animals. Some clever lifting devices used simple pulleys and levers and made it

Earth's Place in the Heavens

One important subject of investigation by early Greek thinkers was the nature and movements of Earth, the Sun, and other heavenly bodies. They all recognized that Earth is a sphere. Most, however, incorrectly concluded that Earth rests at the center of the universe. Aristotle and others proposed that a series of invisible spheres lie beyond the stationary Earth, each nested inside another. One sphere held the Moon, another the Sun, and so forth. Another Greek, Philotus, rejected this geocentric, or Earth-centered, view. He suggested that Earth is just another planet. It and the other heavenly bodies, including the Sun, move around a "central fire," he said. Philotus had the right basic idea, even if some of his details were wrong. Later, Aristarchus of Samos recognized the truth—that Earth and other planets move around the Sun. This helio-centric, or Sun-centered, view was too far ahead of its time, however. Most Greeks, Romans, and other premodern peoples continued to accept the geocentric view.

possible to raise massive blocks of stone to the upper levels of temples and other large buildings. These hoists still required teams of oxen or gangs of slaves to operate, however. The levers and pulleys only reduced the number of animals or men needed to complete the job.

Travel was similarly laborious. People either walked; rode horses, donkeys, or wagons; or sailed or rowed ships. As a result, trips could take days, weeks, or occasionally months. Traveling by land in Greece was particularly difficult. There were only a handful of paved roads, all of them short, during the classical age. Most roads were of dirt, which turned to mud when it rained. This greatly hindered and slowed the pace of travel.

Another difficulty of travel was the danger of highwaymen—thieves and murderers who laid in wait for victims on lonely stretches of road. The Greeks had a number of old tales about such criminals. The Athenians liked to tell how their national hero, Theseus, "made the road safe from villainous highwaymen," as one Greek writer put it. "He overcame Periphetes . . . who, because of the club he carried, was called the club-bearer. . . . [He] used it to kill passers-by. After he took the club away from him, Theseus continued to carry it himself."[11] Few Greek travelers were as strong or brave as Theseus. When possible, therefore, people traveled with companions. These difficulties and dangers that Greek travelers faced were only a few of many that existed before the introduction of modern technology.

Opposite Page: One of the most traveled roads in Greece led to Olympia, site of the Olympic Games.

Notes

Chapter 1: Social Classes and Citizenship

1. Quoted in Mary R. Lefkowitz and Maureen B. Fant, eds., *Women's Life in Greece and Rome: A Source Book in Translation*. Baltimore: Johns Hopkins University Press, 1992, p. 59.
2. Quoted in Lefkowitz and Fant, *Women's Life in Greece and Rome*, p. 64.
3. Plutarch, *Life of Lycurgus*, in *Plutarch on Sparta*, trans. Richard J.A. Talbert. New York: Penguin, 1988, p. 27.

Chapter 2: Families and Their Houses

4. Plutarch, *Life of Agis*, in *Plutarch on Sparta*, p. 58.
5. Plato, *Symposium*, trans. Tom Grittith. Berkeley and Los Angeles: University of California Press, 1985, pp. 176–77.

Chapter 3: Religious Beliefs and Customs

6. Plato, *Timaeus*, in *The Dialogues of Plato*, trans. Benjamin Jowett. Chicago: Encyclopaedia Britannica, 1952, p. 447.
7. Pindar, *Nemean Odes*, in *Pindar: The Odes*, trans. C.'M. Bowra. New York: Penguin, 1969, p. 206.
8. Demosthenes, *On the Crown*, in *The Classical Greek Reader*, ed. Kenneth J. Atchity. New York: Oxford University Press, 1996, pp. 218–19.
9. Quoted in Plato, *Phaedrus*, in *Dialogues of Plato*, p. 141.

Chapter 4: Greek Science and Technology

10. Lucretius, *The Nature of the Universe*, trans. Ronald Latham. Baltimore: Penguin, 1951, p. 29.
11. Apollodorus, *Library*, in *Classical Gods and Heroes*, trans. Rhoda A. Hendricks. New York: Morrow Quill, 1974, p. 170.

Glossary

acropolis: "The city's high place"; a central hill around which many Greek towns were built. The capitalized version—Acropolis—refers to the one in Athens.

agoge: The harsh system of military training undergone by young men in Sparta.

aqueduct: A stone channel that carried water from a lake or stream to a town.

astai: Citizens who lacked political rights. The term most often referred to women.

atimos: A person who lost his or her citizenship.

brazier: A metal container that burned charcoal.

candelabra: A decorative stand that held several candles.

cistern: A tank for catching and storing rainwater.

city-state: A small nation built around a central town.

cosmos: As the Greeks saw it, an orderly system that operated under the influence of natural laws.

exedra: A sitting room opening directly into the courtyard of a house.

fountain house: A small structure that featured stone tanks for storing water from a nearby stream.

geocentric: Earth-centered.

grammatistes: Teachers.

hearth: A fireplace or open oven.

heliocentric: Sun-centered.

helots: Spartan slaves.

isonomia: Equality under the law.

maia: A midwife.

metics: Foreigners living in ancient Athens. They had no political rights.

oikos: The family.

pantheon: A group of gods worshipped by a people.

patron: A god or goddess thought to provide special protection to a city.

phyle (plural **phtylai**): A tribe.

physis: Nature's underlying principle.

Spartiates: Spartan citizens.

symposium: An after-dinner drinking party.

For More Information

Books

Peter Connolly, *The Greek Armies*. Morristown, NJ: Silver Burdette, 1979. A fine, detailed study of Greek armor, weapons, and battle tactics, filled with colorful, accurate illustrations. Highly recommended.

Linda Honan, *Spend the Day in Ancient Greece: Projects and Activities That Bring the Past to Life*. Hoboken, NJ: John Wiley, 1998. An informative and entertaining workbook that instructs children in such hands-on projects as making their own ancient Greek garments.

Don Nardo, *Greek Mythology*. San Diego: KidHaven, 2002. A brief but informative overview of some of the major Greek myths.

———, *Women of Ancient Greece*. San Diego: Lucent Books, 2000. A detailed look at all aspects of the lives of women in the ancient Greek city-states. Although somewhat challenging, it is still accessible to grade-school readers.

Susan Peach and Anne Millard, *The Greeks*. London: Usborne, 1990. A general overview of the history, culture, myths, and everyday life of ancient Greece, presented in a format suitable to young, basic readers.

Jonathon Rutland, *See Inside an Ancient Greek Town*. New York: Barnes and Noble, 1995. This colorful introduction to ancient Greek life is aimed at basic readers.

Websites

A Day in the Life of an Ancient Greek, Hellenic Museum and Cultural Center (www.hellenicmuseum.org/gallery/ancient%;20greek.htm).
A useful, easy-to-read general source for ancient Greek life, including clothes, food, sports, art, and more.

Everyday Life in Ancient Greece, That's Greece
(www.thatsgreece.com/online/section.asp?section = 10).
A student-friendly site about ancient Greek society created for English-speaking countries by a group of Greek writers based in Athens. It has links to topics such as houses, marriage and divorce, slaves, clothes, education, food and drink, farming, and more.

Greek Costume Through the Ages: Ancient Greece, Institute of International Education School Program
(www.annaswebart.com/culture/costhistory/ancient/index.html).
This informative site, which explores the everyday clothes worn in ancient Greece, is supplemented by helpful drawings and photos.

Perseus Project, Tufts University Department of the Classics
(www.perseus.tufts.edu).
The most comprehensive and respected general source about ancient Greece on the Internet. Contains hundreds of links to all aspects of Greek history, life, and culture; supported by numerous photos of artifacts. Highly recommended for all.

Index

Picture Credits

About the Author

Historian Don Nardo has published many volumes about ancient Greece, its history, and its culture, among them *Leaders of Ancient Greece*, *A Travel Guide to Ancient Athens*, and *The Ancient Greeks*. He lives in Massachusetts with his wife, Christine.